Pebble

Great African

T0101120

# Garrett
# MORGAN

by Sarah L. Schuette

Content Consultant: Allen Ballard, Professor,
History and Africana Studies, University at Albany

Consulting Editor: Gail Saunders-Smith, PhD

CAPSTONE PRESS
a capstone imprint

Pebble Books are published by Capstone Press,
1710 Roe Crest Drive, North Mankato, Minnesota 56003
www.capstonepub.com

**Library of Congress Cataloging-in-Publication Data**
Schuette, Sarah L., 1976–
  Garrett Morgan / by Sarah L. Schuette.
    pages cm. — (Pebble Books. Great African-Americans)
  Includes bibliographical references and index.
  Summary: "Simple text and photographs present the life of Garrett Morgan, an African-American
inventor and entrepreneur"— Provided by publisher.
  ISBN 978-1-4914-0504-8 (library binding) — ISBN 978-1-4914-0510-9 (pbk.) — ISBN 978-1-
4914-0516-1 (ebook pdf)
1.  Morgan, Garrett A., 1877–1963—Juvenile literature. 2.  African American inventors—
Biography—Juvenile literature. 3.  African American businesspeople—Biography—Juvenile
literature.  I. Title.
  TJ140.M67S38 2015
  609.2–dc23
  [B]                                        2014007344

**Editorial Credits**
Nikki Bruno Clapper, editor; Terri Poburka, designer; Kelly Garvin, media researcher;
Laura Manthe, production specialist

**Photo Credits**
AP Images: AP Photo, 10; Cleveland Press Collections: courtesy of the Michael Schwartz Library
Special Collections, Cleveland State University, 12; Cleveland Public Library: Photograph Collection,
20; Getty Images/Archive Photos: cover, 18; Library of Congress: 8; Shutterstock: Marfo, design
element; The New York Public Library: The Miriam and Ira D. Wallach Division of Art, Prints and
Photographs: Photography Collection, 6; Wikimedia: 4, 14, US Patent and Trademark Office, 16

## Note to Parents and Teachers

The Great African-Americans set supports national curriculum standards for
social studies related to people, places, and environments. This book describes and
illustrates Garrett Morgan. The images support early readers in understanding
the text. The repetition of words and phrases helps early readers learn new words.
This book also introduces early readers to subject-specific vocabulary words, which
are defined in the Glossary section. Early readers may need assistance to read
some words and to use the Table of Contents, Glossary, Read More, Internet Sites,
Critical Thinking Using the Common Core, and Index sections of the book.

# Table of Contents

1877
born

# Early Years

Garrett Morgan was a famous inventor. He was born in Kentucky in 1877. Garrett had 10 brothers and sisters. His parents were freed slaves.

*a street in Cleveland, 1901*

1877

born

Garrett left school after

sixth grade. At age 14

he moved to Ohio in search

of a job. Garrett settled

in the city of Cleveland.

He worked at a sewing

machine company.

a sewing machine company

1877
born

1907
opens repair
shop

8

# Grown-Up Garrett

Garrett studied machines
all day at work. He invented
a new sewing machine
and a belt fastener. In 1907
he opened a repair shop
for sewing equipment.

**1877**

born

**1907**

opens repair
shop

**1908**

marries Mary
Anne Hassek

In 1908 Garrett married

Mary Anne Hassek.

Garrett and Mary Anne

opened a tailor shop.

Garrett also sold a cream

that straightened hair.

He became wealthy.

aring
nood

1907
opens repair
shop

1908
marries Mary
Anne Hassek

# Middle Years

Garrett's most famous invention was a safety hood. It helped firefighters breathe safely in smoky air. Garrett's safety hood saved many lives. Soldiers used it during World War I.

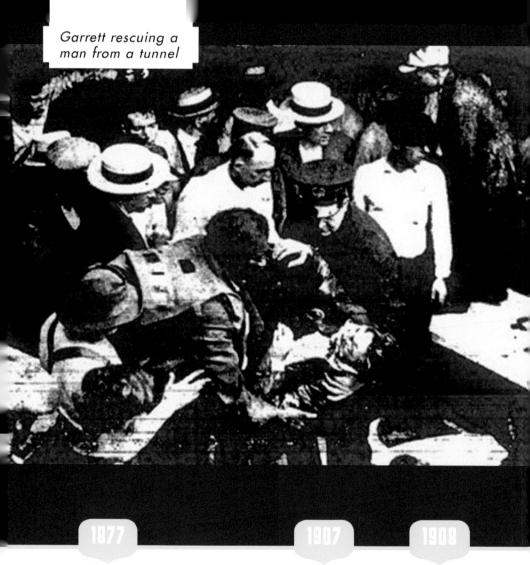

*Garrett rescuing a man from a tunnel*

**1877**
born

**1907**
opens repair shop

**1908**
marries Mary Anne Hassek

In 1916 there was an explosion in a tunnel under Lake Erie. Garrett and his brother rushed to the tunnel. They put on safety hoods, went into the tunnel, and saved two men's lives.

**1916**

saves men
in tunnel

Nov. 20, 1923.

G. A. MORGAN

TRAFFIC SIGNAL

Filed Feb. 27. 1922

1,475,024

2 Sheets-Sheet 1

FIG.-2

FIG.-3

FIG.-4

FIG.-1

INVENTOR

Garrett A. Morgan,

By ........ Macklin,

ATTORNEYS

's

nal

1907

opens repair
shop

190

marries
Anne H

In the 1920s there were a lot
of car accidents. Garrett wanted
the streets to be safer. In 1923
he invented a traffic signal.
His signals later became the
traffic lights we use today.

1916
saves men
in tunnel

1923
invents traffic
signal

1877
born

1907
opens repair shop

1908
marries Mary Anne Hassek

# Later Years

Garrett was a leader in the
African-American community.
He started a newspaper
called the *Cleveland Call.*
He also gave money to
African-American colleges.

**1916**

saves men
in tunnel

**1923**

invents traffic
signal

1877
born

1907
opens repair
shop

1908
marries Mary
Anne Hassek

After a lifetime of inventing, Garrett died in 1963. He is best known for his safety hood and traffic signal. These inventions made the world a safer place.

1916
saves men
in tunnel

1923
invents traffic
signal

1963
dies

# Glossary

community—a group of people who live in the same area

explosion—a moment when something blows apart with a loud bang and great force

fastener—something that attaches two things to each other

invent—to think up and make something new

inventor—a person who thinks up and makes something new

settle—to make a place your home

slave—a person who is owned by another person

tailor—a person who sews clothing

World War I (1914–1918)—the war between the Central Powers (Germany, Austria-Hungary, and Turkey) and the Allied Powers (mainly France, Great Britain, Russia, Italy, Japan, and the United States)

# Read More

**Abdul-Jabbar, Kareem.** *What Color Is My World?: The Lost History of African-American Inventors.* Somerville, Mass.: Candlewick, 2012.

**Greenfield, Eloise.** *The Great Migration: Journey to the North.* New York: Amistad, 2011.

**Ready, Dee.** *Firefighters Help.* Pebble Books: Our Community Helpers. North Mankato, Minn.: Capstone Press, 2013.

## Critical Thinking Using the Common Core

1. What kinds of businesses did Garrett Morgan start? (Key Ideas and Details)

2. What kinds of information about Garrett Morgan can you find in the chapter called "Early Years"? (Craft and Structure)

# Index

Word Count: 257
Grade: 1
Early-Intervention Level: 22